World of wines as roses
he same name there is
e, of delic...   ...ody, of
es pleas...   ...them,
leave yo...   ...ing. "

ESTATES MA...   ...ANCE

"Chardonnay, this rich, buttery wine, marries perfectly with a tart tomato salad."

ALICE WATERS
RESTAURATEUR, CHEZ PANISSE, BERKELEY, CALIFORNIA

Chardonnay

Chardonnay

PHOTOGRAPHS FROM AROUND THE WORLD

created and photographed by
CHARLES O'REAR

text by
MICHAEL CREEDMAN

foreword by
MARGRIT BIEVER MONDAVI

SMITHMARK

PRODUCED WITH SUPPORT FROM CORBIS

This edition published in 1999 by SMITHMARK Publishers, a division of U.S. Media Holdings, Inc., 115 West 18th Street, New York, NY 10011.

SMITHMARK books are available for bulk purchase for sales promotion and premium use. For details write or call the manager of special sales, SMITHMARK Publishers, 115 West 18th Street, New York, NY 10011; 212-519-1300.

Produced by Jennifer Barry Design, Sausalito, California
Design by Jennifer Barry and Leslie Anne Barry
Edited by Blake Hallanan
Layout Production by Kristen Wurz
Consultants: Randle Johnson, Michael Silacci, Elias Fernandez
Picture Editor: Laura Hunt

Charles O'Rear's photographs can be viewed at www.winephotos.com

Photographs by Charles O'Rear, ©1999 Corbis, see page 143.

All photographs in this book are available for sale from Corbis. Orders can be placed to Corbis at 800-260-0444, or online at www.corbisimages.com. All photographs were scanned on a high-resolution Heidelberg Tango and can be purchased electronically.

Library of Congress Cataloging-in-Publication Data
O'Rear, Charles, 1941–
Chardonnay : photographs from around the world / Charles O'Rear ;
foreword by Margrit Biever Mondavi.
p.   cm.
Includes index.
ISBN: 0-7651-1028-8 (alk. paper)
1. Chardonnay (Wine)--Pictorial works.
2. Wine and winemaking--Pictorial works.   I. Title.
TP548.O59   1999
641.2'222--dc21   98-37641
CIP

Printed in Hong Kong
10 9 8 7 6 5 4 3 2 1

PRECEDING PAGES: Arranged in the style of a stately English country garden, the orderly vines of the Petaluma Winery outside Adelaide, Australia, soak up the Southern Hemisphere sun in February; Chardonnay grapes; Vines spreading through the Carneros region near Napa; The hands of a French vineyard worker scratched and scarred from pruning chardonnay vines in Chablis; Sparkling wine bottles await labels at the Argyle Winery in Oregon.

contents

foreword

BY MARGRIT BIEVER MONDAVI

I was touched and enormously pleased when Chuck O'Rear asked me to write the introduction to his new book, *Chardonnay*. I have admired him and his work since he was our neighbor in St. Helena and I saw his beautiful photography book on the Napa Valley. Following the publication of his most recent book on Cabernet, which my husband Robert prefaced, this book is a perfect follow-up. After all, how better to sing the praises of the queen of all wines than by photographing her many moods and faces?

This grape, which probably originated centuries ago in the Burgundy region of France, is now grown on many continents. Today, Chardonnay has become one of the most popular white wines for, above all other wines, it yields a wide spectrum of flavors that range from the lighter, fruitier style to rich-golden buttery tastes.

Chardonnay is a wine I enjoy so much, whether it suggests a hint of apple, tropical fruit, chamomile or banana—and almost always with a kiss of oak from aging in wood barrels. I drink Chardonnay when I am sad because it lifts my spirits and I drink it when I am happy because it makes me even happier.

Robert Mondavi Winery produced its first Chardonnay in 1966, the same year our winery was built in Oakville, California. Later, in the mid '70s we started fermenting in wood barrels and experimenting with how to best balance the oak flavor in wine. Today, Chardonnay is one of our most elegant wines. Our Napa Valley Chardonnay comes from the cooler regions of Carneros, south of Napa, while our Byron Winery near Santa Maria, California, produces the wine with a flavor of its soil and climate. In the San Joaquin Valley we produce our Woodbridge Chardonnay, a popular, simpler style wine, and now we have gone to Chile to produce a Chardonnay with yet another personality.

In this beautiful book, Charles O'Rear has a third eye and a sixth sense when he captures the moments, the scene, and the pulse of Chardonnay with his camera. He travelled to regions of the world where this noble grape is grown and the wine is produced. He understands the subtle differences expressed by soil and climate. He appreciates the vintner's art and the important part that barrel aging plays. I lift my glass in a toast to Chuck for this wonderful book. It is a book to cherish, along with a glass of the queen of wines—Chardonnay.

Boxes of just-picked chardonnay grapes are kept cool until they can be
crushed at Spring Creek Vineyard in St. Helena, California.

introduction

BY CHARLES O' REAR

Can photographs capture the complexity of wine, especially a wine as popular and loved as Chardonnay? Is it possible to go beyond a pretty glass, a picturesque vineyard, or a winemaker posed with his barrels? Can you find the underlying truths that stir our emotions and excite our palates?

Those were the questions I asked several years ago when this project was first taking shape. Now, it seems that the answer clearly is yes.

This book goes beyond the glass, the vineyard, and the winemaker to what might be described as the soul of Chardonnay. It is my attempt to express in pictures and words the essence of this exceptional wine. Moreover, I want to explore the capacity that Chardonnay has to spark passion. It's a passion you can see in the dedication of winemakers, of the people who work in the vineyard, and the delight of the millions of people all over the world who have fallen in love with Chardonnay.

My own affair with wine began in 1966 during a visit to a home winemaking shop in Santa Barbara, California. At first I was simply curious about whether there was more than simple chemistry in the way this lowly grape was transformed into a majestic libation. How did it become a wine that feels like a woman's skin, tastes like fine spun gold, and reflects an amazing yellow-green color that reminds me simultaneously of the promise of springtime and the lush fullness of summer?

But at that time, Chardonnay had not entered the lives of Americans. Instead, they were drinking something called "Chablis." Unfortunately, the wine that was in those bottles labeled "Chablis" had nothing to do with the fabulous French wine of that name. It was only a few years later, in the '70s, that the great wineries of northern California began experimenting with Chardonnay. The California vintners knew chardonnay grapes had made the world's greatest white wines in France for centuries. So they figured, why couldn't they grow chardonnay grapes for wine in their own vineyards? Their attempts proved to be very successful.

Working backstage in the wine world for twenty years has provided me a unique perspective. My role as a journalist has allowed me to meet and get to know many of the winery owners, winemakers, and field workers in the industry. My desire was to present their knowledge and experience through this first photography book devoted entirely to Chardonnay—from its birth to its consumption.

The photographs in this volume were made at various times during my career. Some date back to my *National Geographic* assignments. Many more are from a personal project to document life in the Napa Valley. Most recently, this project has enjoyed the financial support of Bill Gates' privately owned company, Corbis, the electronic archive that contracted me to follow wine harvests around the world.

After flying more than 100,000 miles and shooting nearly 100,000 photos on wine, I'm just beginning to understand why Chardonnay can be so great and so popular, just as I'm getting a handle on how a jet engine can lift a Boeing 747 into the air. I understand now, too, that I enjoy Chardonnay the most when I share it with friends in a welcoming environment.

I have no favorites and I have found no bad Chardonnay in the world, only a wine ranging from good to great. On some days I may wish for a creamy California-style, which has the touch of new oak barrels, or on other days I will want the traditional French-style, which usually has only the flavors of the grape and the soil. Many wine drinkers have not had the same experiences, though, so they must choose their Chardonnay based on name recognition, attractive label, store display, reputation, or price.

The number of Chardonnay labels is likely to keep growing. Thousands of acres of new chardonnay vineyards continue to be planted every year, winemakers continue to experiment with new techniques, and winery owners are expanding into each other's native countries.

It's understandable why wine is popular — it's been around since ancient civilizations. And the word *wine* appears in the Bible more than 200 times. Today, wine is a huge business with annual U.S. sales at more than $16 billion, as reported by the San Francisco Wine Institute. Worldwide, about 10 million bottles are opened on any given day.

That's a lot of wine, confirming my view that wine in general and Chardonnay in particular are here to stay. My hope is that this book will expand the ways in which it can be understood and enjoyed.

WASHINGTON

OREGON

CALIFORNIA

FRANCE

SPAIN

CHILE

Chardonnay vines can grow in most of the world's temperate zones. These nine are among the regions that have proved they have the climate and soil needed to produce distinguished vintages. Chardonnay grapes don't grow well in the tropics and are only beginning to be cultivated in Asia.

SOUTH AFRICA

AUSTRALIA

NEW ZEALAND

chapter one
CHARDONNAY

the grape

In all the world, in all its forms, the chardonnay grape fills more wine bottles than any other.

Chardonnay is the vine that produces the glorious French Chablis. It is the grape in more than 3,000 Chardonnay brands around the globe. And chardonnay is the grape preferred by makers of fine Champagne and sparkling wine.

Surely, Chardonnay is a much loved wine. And because it presents itself in so many attractive forms, some consider it the most romantic member of the wine family. But it's not a hopeless, heedless romantic. Instead, it is a queen of wines, distinguished by style and elegance.

Chardonnay, even in its most subtle and complex mood, is a very accessible wine. You don't need a graduate degree in wine science to appreciate its richness, complexity, depth of flavor, and many different styles. It ranges from a deep, rich taste with hints of oak, butter, and vanilla—all the way to crisp or fruity wines that are more delicate with tastes of apple, peach, or melon.

On the vine, the ripe chardonnay grape is a rich yellow-green. In theory, it can grow in temperate regions all over the world, but there are less than a dozen regions that have developed a reputation for outstanding Chardonnay.

Chardonnay probably gets its name from a town in the Burgundy region near where some of the more distinguished vintages, such as Montrachet and Meursault, originate. Scholars speculate that the grape either mutated in France from pinot noir or was brought from the Middle East by the Romans 2,000 years ago.

Grape vines are most vulnerable to weather during spring and fall, when early frost or late rain can ruin a crop. In March or April, the danger comes just as the buds break out from the vines. Chardonnay is in special jeopardy because bud break, the first emergence of growth, appears early in the season, when the threat from frost is greatest. An entire crop can be lost if the temperature dips below 28 degrees and the vines are not protected. Not surprisingly, vineyard masters have adopted a variety of frost-beating techniques. These include oil heaters that fire up in the predawn cold, wind machines that circulate warmer upper level air toward the ground, and water sprays that protect the delicate buds by forming ice sheaths around them.

In the fall, the key danger to the chardonnay grape is rain. If the vines are soaked before the grapes are mature enough to be picked, trapped moisture in the heavy clusters can foster various forms of fungi.

In order to harvest grapes in the fall that have the flavor and sugar levels needed to make great wine, the grower makes a number of critical decisions during the year. Among them are how to manage the canopy of leaves and berries on the vines and how to train the vines. Most growers try to expose chardonnay grape clusters to the sun and moderate the density of grape leaves. Although it may look luxuriantly productive to casual observers, vineyard masters know now that too much foliage can lead to fungus infestation and uneven grape ripening.

Even if the weather cooperates, the grapes must be also be protected from animals such as rabbits, deer, squirrels, rodents, and birds, which eat the buds, bark, and canes.

Despite these dangers, there's usually a happy ending when summer ends. Most of the time, in most of the vineyards, when the days grow short the vines are full of ripe chardonnay grapes, just waiting for harvest.

This morning's early dew will burn off the ripe grapes before they are
picked for harvest *(above)*. Chardonnay grapes in the shade of the vine's leaf canopy
are almost ripe. Grapes that receive direct sun ripen faster *(preceding pages)*.

Winter pruning at the Robert Mondavi Vineyard in the Carneros
region of northern California prepares the vines for vigorous growth in spring *(left)*.
In the fall, bud chips from chardonnay vines are grafted onto hardy rootstock,
a plant which forms the root system of all grapevines. They will lie dormant over
winter and then grow into a 6-foot vine by the end of the season *(above)*.

In Oregon's Dundee Hills region southwest of
Portland, the spring's first growth of weeds is mowed instead of
plowed under because plowed ground heats faster *(left)*.
Warm earth would stimulate buds to emerge prematurely.
These wind machines in the Napa Valley help
keep the frost away from delicate chardonnay buds, which are
susceptible to subfreezing weather *(above)*. The grapes
from a vineyard near Beaune, France, have been picked, pressed
and put into barrels to ferment *(preceding pages)*.

Every wine-growing region has a different method of pruning. In France the pruned canes are burned because the stony soil of this vineyard won't easily break down shredded stems into compost as they do in more fertile fields *(top left)*. Vineyard workers like this one in Burgundy check to assure that all the pruning debris has been cleared *(left)*. If dead vegetation is not plowed under, it can harbor fungi and insects. New vines planted in translucent growth tubes in the Adelaide Hills region of Australia will begin to bear fruit in three years *(above)*. These tubes became popular throughout the world during the 1990s because they increase the percentage of grafted chardonnay vines that survive transplanting.

Although most vines produce grapes in two or three years, full production isn't achieved until the fourth or fifth year. Here, a worker inspects new chardonnay vines to be planted in the cool hills north of San Francisco Bay *(left)*. After machines make precision connections between rootstock and cuttings from chardonnay vines called scion canes, the graft is tightly wrapped and then dipped in a protective wax *(above)*. Moistened and stored for a few weeks in a warm "callusing room," the grafted parts join together. Then, they go to cool storage until ready for planting in the spring.

Once the first emergence of growth called bud
break begins in the spring, the vines are susceptible to early
morning frosts. Oil-fired heaters in the Carneros region
of northern California warm the buds just enough to keep
them healthy *(above)*. Growers claim that the blanket
of summer fog typically hanging over the fertile Napa Valley
protects the region from California's intense morning sun
and thus produces a better chardonnay grape than can be grown
in the sunnier interior *(right)*. Bud break in the Dundee Hills of
Oregon is the time when dormant vines come alive *(following pages)*.
The canes are secured to the trellis wire in the popular
"Double Guyot" alignment invented in the nineteenth century
by Dr. Jules Guyot, a pioneering French viticulturist.

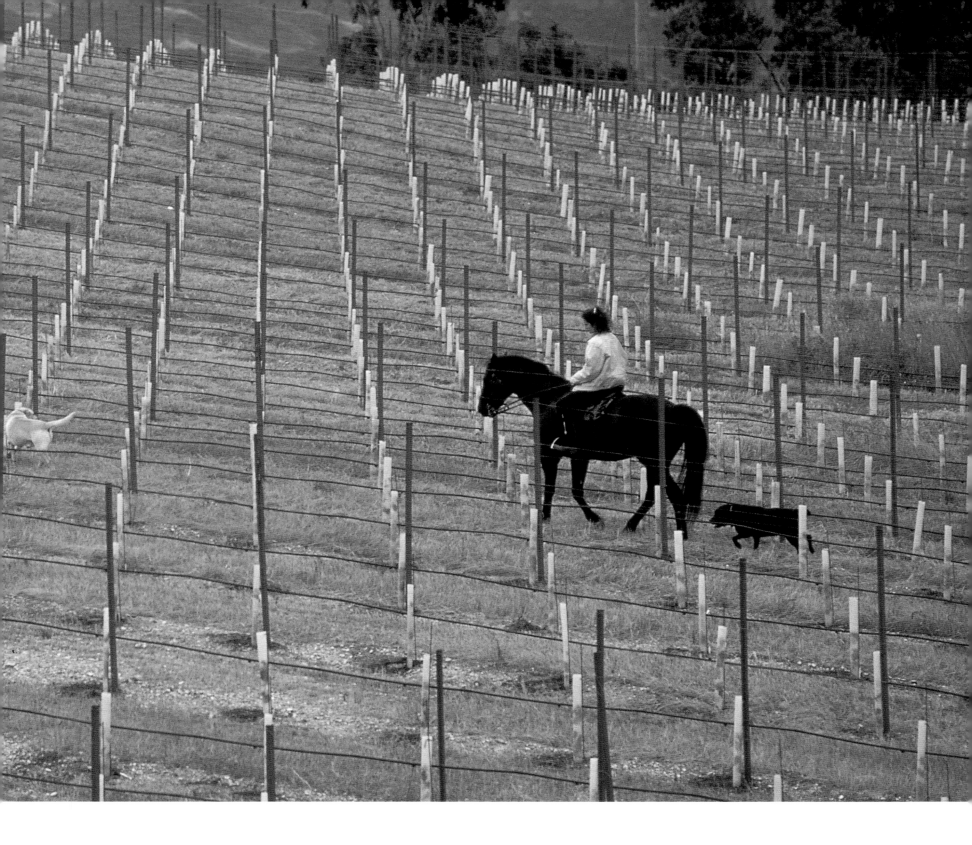

In the Napa Valley region of northern California, Far Niente Winery's nineteenth-century architecture recalls a different era *(top left)*. Today, one of the most preferred wines chosen by visitors there is Chardonnay. In southern California, a ranch owner on horseback inspects her newly replanted vineyard near Santa Barbara *(above)*. But other riders are not so lucky. In this region, the popularity of Chardonnay has sparked a competition for acreage between new vineyards and other land uses, such as riding trails. Plastic growth tubes protect newly planted vines from deer and rabbits, and damage from weed spray during the fragile first year of growth *(left)*.

The first grape leaves emerge from the dormant vines in early spring, gathering energy from the sun to make sugars in the vine. In about six weeks, the first blossoms will appear *(above)*. No bees needed. Grape blossoms pollinate themselves and thus don't need bright petals or heavy perfumes to attract bees or birds *(right)*. Vineyard workers at Cambria Winery in the Santa Maria Valley of California sucker (trim) the growing vines *(top right)*. Scarves are worn to protect against windburn that prevails in that region. Chardonnay cuttings have been grafted to vigorous rootstock and planted in tiny nursery pots at the Cottage Garden Nursery in St. Helena, California *(far right)*. They will soon be transplanted into a vineyard, where during the first summer the vines may grow as much as an inch a day. Thousands of cases of the world's finest Champagne will be made from the chardonnay grapes of this vineyard in northern France *(following pages)*.

Cork oaks typically live over 150 years. A venerable Mediterranean cork oak tree in Portugal has its outer bark stripped by an experienced crew who take care not to damage the living inner bark *(left)*. The exterior bark will grow back and be ready for harvesting again in nine years. After the bark is stripped, it is stacked and aged outside, then boiled in water to remove pests and make it more flexible. Then it is trimmed into slabs from which cork bottle stoppers are cut *(above)*.

The sun rising in the east over these vines at Coldstream Hills near Melbourne, Australia will dry the dew from the grapes early, preventing attack by fungi *(above)*. Voracious birds in parts of Australia demand special consideration, like this elaborate scarecrow, to keep them from eating the crop before it can be picked *(top right)*. Dissected, the chardonnay grape reveals its distinctive seed shape *(far right)*. If seeds are crushed into the juice, the wine will become bitter. Chardonnay grapes glow in a spotlight on a dark night in St. Helena, just before harvest *(following page)*.

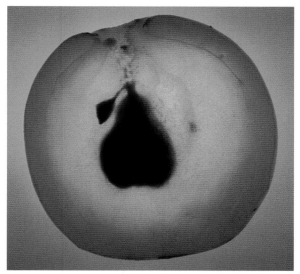

"Great Chardonnay is exotic, an elixir of folded spices, cold stone and pome fruits and suave texture conferred by its pedigree. No other white variety gets close to its profound complexity."

BRIAN CROSER
PETALUMA WINERY, PICCADILLY, SOUTH AUSTRALIA

chapter two
CHARDONNAY

the harvest

CHARDONNAY: THE HARVEST

After a tranquil summer of pruning and trimming the vineyard, harvest season in Chardonnay country begins as suddenly as the first plunge of a roller coaster. It's scary, it's exciting, and as long as nothing goes wrong, it's a delight.

But the grape harvest is more than a thrill ride. It's the culmination of at least a year's work and the beginning of a barrel and tank adventure that will require constant attention for another year or more.

One of the most difficult decisions for a winemaker is exactly when to pick the grapes. That's especially true with chardonnay because the flavors are so much more subtle than in red wines. As grapes ripen, the concentration of flavor-making fruit acids declines and the proportion of alcohol-making sugars increases. The decision of exactly when to take the grapes from the vines is critical.

To make Champagne and similar sparkling wines, the grapes are picked before they develop much sugar. Although not terribly tasty to eat, the greenish fruit has a high acid content that can withstand years of bottle aging in Champagne cellars.

For traditional French Chablis, the chardonnay grapes are also harvested early, to ensure its characteristic crispness.

For other Chardonnay wines, the harvest decision depends on other factors of taste including whether the winemaker intends to produce Chardonnay that is fruity or full bodied.

The actual process at harvest is simple: ripe grapes are picked and cleaned to remove what's known in the field as MOG (Material Other than Grapes). Then the grapes are crushed to release the juice, which in the wine business is called "must." Finally, the "must" goes into tanks, vats, or barrels for fermentation. Unlike red wines, where the skins and seeds that determine most of the wine's flavor stay with the juice, the chardonnay "must" contains only the juice and some crushed pulp. There are no seeds or skins.

Although mechanical picking is much faster, most premium chardonnay grapes are harvested by hand. Machines can bruise the grape skins, which degrades the juice. The pickers take care not to pick bunches that contain unripe or rotted grapes.

An experienced vineyard worker can pick 1 or 2 tons of grapes a day, depending on whether the grape clusters are dense and whether the vines are well trimmed. The clusters are not yanked off the vines, but instead are cleanly snipped with shears or cut with a sharp curved knife.

Most chardonnay grapes have to be picked early in the morning, before the sun's rays heat the vines, because once the grapes are off the vine, air and bacteria affect the chemistry of the juice. High temperatures can turn the chardonnay grape juice brown very quickly. Oxidation occurs half as fast at 72 degrees as it does at 90 degrees. Juice kept at 54 degrees degenerates only one-quarter as much as at 90 degrees. Bacteria that turn wine into vinegar also are more active when the temperatures are high.

Harvesting when it's cool is especially important if the winery where the grapes are pressed is any distance from the vineyard. During harvest, many winemakers will simply suspend picking for the day if the field temperature rises too high.

When the grapes have been picked and crushed, the first plunge of the roller coaster ride experience connected with the harvest is over. But the wine and the winemaker will experience plenty of ups and downs before this vintage of Chardonnay is safely in bottles and ready to drink.

The shape of the chardonnay grape leaf is distinct from other varieties *(above)*.
Leaf shape differentiation is one of the techniques used in ampelography, the science of
identifying and describing of the varieties of *Vitis*, the vine genus that produces wine grapes.
A Chilean picker takes home a sample at quitting time *(preceding pages)*.

Early in the season at Rippon Vineyard on New Zealand's South Island, bird netting is unrolled across the top of the vines to protect
them from a huge population of birds that eat the crop. As grapes are picked in each section, the netting is removed for repair and storage *(above)*.
Elsewhere, silvery reflecting tape, sound blasters, traps, and cats are used to control the birds. Although expensive, the netting is the most
effective and environmentally benign control method. As the chardonnay grapes ripen toward harvest, a Chilean viticulturist checks sugar content with
a refractometer *(right)*. After collecting samples, the winemaker will crush these grapes in the lab and test carefully for the level of hydrogen ions,
the concentration of food acids, and the proportion of sugar in the juice *(top right)*. Only a ridge away from the Pacific Ocean near San Luis Obispo,
California, the Edna Valley, in the shadow of Islay Hill, enjoys a relatively cool growing season that favors chardonnay grapes *(preceding pages)*.

Chilean pickers haul their equipment to begin the harvest of vines they've tended for almost a year *(above)*.

Migratory pickers from the Pacific islands of Tonga wear wide-brimmed hats at harvest near Auckland *(top right)*.

A sharpening stone is vitally important to a California grape picker because his distinctive curved cutter must

be sharpened several times a day *(right)*.

A mechanical picker is used to harvest chardonnay grapes in Washington state *(above)*. Most premium grapes are handpicked by a team of skilled workers, as here in the Champagne region of France, because they are less likely than mechanical methods to crush the grape skins and cause partial oxidation of the juice *(right)*.

Working quickly and with deep respect for the quality of the grapes, good pickers everywhere look similar. These workers near Barcelona, Spain, are hard to distinguish from those who bring in the chardonnay harvest in Burgundy or Napa or the other premier regions of the world *(above)*. The urgent goal at harvest is to pick the ripe fruit gently and rush it to the crusher whether in Napa, California *(right)*; Martinsborough, New Zealand *(above right)*; or in Chablis, France *(far right)*.

Lugging a load of about 55 pounds, this Chilean harvest worker has another 40 feet to trudge before he can empty his picking box into a large container that will transport grapes back to the winery *(left)*.

Wine has been made in Chile since the sixteenth century when Spanish conquistadors introduced grape vines. Traditional hats do double duty in Chilean vineyards: protecting workers from the intense sunlight while picking and then cushioning the load when hauling *(above)*. A pair of tractors pulls a mechanical picking machine and a grape gondola through a chardonnay vineyard in Australia's Barossa Valley *(right)*.

Teamwork makes the picking go faster at this Miguel Torres vineyard near Barcelona, Spain *(left)*. Enjoying a joke together, friends take a break from picking in the Chablis region before lunch *(above)*.

The castle of a neighboring Spanish winery
overlooks this chardonnay vineyard as harvesting
begins. The leaf canopy, which is the way the
vines are trained and trimmed, is chosen by each
vineyard director according to the type of
grapes, the rainfall, the composition of the soil,
and the personal preferences of the owner.
The balance between leaf cover and exposure
of grape clusters to sunlight is an issue of
controversy among winemakers.

At midday, sample grapes from the late morning's picking near Curicó, Chile, go back to the winery along with the supervisors and driver *(above)*. It takes 250 loaded picking boxes to fill this 5-ton gondola with grapes from the harvest *(top right)*. After crushing, fermenting, and aging, it will produce 3,600 bottles of Chardonnay—a bottle a day for ten years. Tourists visiting the wineries are usually welcome, but during harvest, they need to be kept out of the way of trucks and machinery rushing to meet harvest schedules *(right)*.

The last day of harvest near Epernay, France, is celebrated with vines that are draped across
the trucks as they bring in the last load of chardonnay that will go into premium Champagne *(above)*.
Making merry for others is hard work. A worker takes a deep breath as the grape crush
in Champagne comes to an end *(right)*.

Cradled in their individual forty-pound-capacity picking boxes, chardonnay grapes waiting
to be crushed at Mumm Napa Valley are kept in the shade to prevent damage from overheating *(left)*.
In Australia, it takes a forklift to heft a collection box containing a half ton of mechanically
picked grapes into the crusher *(above)*. Although it looks like a meat grinder, this auger is the best
way to move chardonnay grapes gently and quickly to the press *(following pages)*.

A blackboard in Chile is marked with the critical chemical measures of the grapes harvested that day *(above)*. The levels of each will influence the way the winemaker decides to ferment and age the wine. A pair of technicians at the Miguel Torres Winery in Spain haul a sample of the harvest to the lab for analysis *(right)*. Squeezed in a hand-cranked wooden press, the juice from the chardonnay grapes in this home winery in St. Helena can equal the best commercial wine, if it gets the same care and storage advantages *(above right)*. After fermentation at a Napa Valley winery, some topping wine is held in reserve in bottles *(far right)*. This wine is poured into barrels to replace the wine that naturally evaporates through the wood during the aging process.

Cubas 5000 - LTs.
Ascorbico. 5 × 60 = 300
Enzyma 3 × 60 = 180
Sulfuroso = 2,0

For yeast to convert sugar into alcohol, there can't be more than a trace of oxygen in the mixture. Unlike red wine, where floating skins and pulp effectively keep out the oxygen, Chardonnay has no top layer to protect against oxidation. Here at Long Vineyards in St. Helena, water-filled fermentation locks attached to barrels allow carbon dioxide from the fermentation process to escape, but keeps oxygen out *(left)*. A newly painted end post in New Zealand's South Island is testimony to the rapid growth of Chardonnay's popularity *(following page)*.

"Chardonnay is the late bloomer of the sparkling wine world ... tight, acidic, and high-strung when young, but given time it becomes elegant, lean, and focused. Well worth the wait!"

DAWNINE DYER
WINEMAKER, DOMAINE CHANDON, YOUNTVILLE, CALIFORNIA

chapter three
CHARDONNAY

the
wine

For the winemaker, a ripe field of chardonnay is like a giant block of flawless white marble, just waiting to be carved. To a greater extent than perhaps any wine in the world, Chardonnay is an expression of the individual winemaker's art.

"With Cabernet, I'm a shepherd," says one Napa winemaker. "My job is to get the grapes where they're going, but when I make Chardonnay, I am a sculptor."

That doesn't mean that the grapes don't matter. The final product relies heavily on grapes of extremely high quality. And that's one reason Chardonnays tend to be expensive. But growing good grapes is only the beginning.

The winemaker's first big decision is whether the Chardonnay should be crisp and fruity or full bodied and complex. To preserve the fruity tastes, winemakers usually choose to ferment in stainless steel tanks. Fermentation in a new oak barrel will produce a more complex wine with definite accents of the oak.

If it were simply a matter of choosing between tanks and barrels, making Chardonnay would be like playing with clay, not sculpting marble. In fact, there are many more issues for the winemaker, like selecting which yeast will convert the grape sugar into alcohol. Instead of a recognized commercial wine yeast, some winemakers are taking their chances with indigenous yeasts.

Then the winemaker has to decide whether or not to age the wine in the same container as the old yeast cells. It's known as "sur lie" aging, or "on the lees." Some say this technique is what gives some Chardonnay a creamy flavor. Others claim it comes from the oak barrels.

But still others think that richness comes from what's known as malolactic fermentation, where one natural food acid in the wine, malic acid, is converted into a milder compound, lactic acid. The malolactic conversion produces the same flavor element that gives butter its aroma.

At different points during the aging process, the wine may be gently transferred or "racked" from barrel to barrel. The idea is to let the tiny particles of dead yeast, salts, and other impurities settle out to the bottom and then to siphon off only the clear wine to a clean tank or barrel, leaving the sediment in the bottom.

Typically, about a year after the harvest, the aging process is finished. Now the vintage needs to be blended. The wine in each barrel may vary slightly in taste because the grapes come from different locations and their taste is influenced by the soil and microclimates experienced during growth.

On blending day, samples of all the Chardonnays in the winery are tasted by the winemaker, the owners, and a key group of advisors. They agree on how best to blend the wine so they can produce the kind of Chardonnay that represents the winery and the winemaker's intentions.

For the consumer, the result of all these efforts is a range of styles so wide as to be almost bewildering. But that enormous range of choices is a triumph, because with Chardonnay, the entire range of taste possibilities not only exists, but can be fulfilled. All it takes is to buy a bottle and enjoy the many tastes of Chardonnay.

In Spain the castle at Miguel Torres Winery, which now serves as a VIP visitor center, is refracted in a glass of Chardonnay *(above)*. The cellarmaster at Salon Champagne House in Le Mesnil-sur-Oger, France, reflects on the quality of the day's first sample *(preceding pages)*.

Getting ahead on the job, a winery worker in France peers inside a giant blending tank to assure
that all the residues have been removed *(above)*. Chardonnay can be made without barrel fermentation, as samples
from stainless steel tanks in Australia's Hunter Valley reveal *(right)*. Insiders in the trade refer to the
enormous tanks in which Chardonnay is blended before bottling as "the pots and pans of winemaking" *(top right)*.

A stainless steel "wine thief" will be used to suction a sample from a barrel at Peter Lehmann Wines in Australia *(left)*. Frequent tasting and testing of barrel contents are vital to assure the fermentation and aging process is proceeding well. Winemakers at Stag's Leap Wine Cellars in Napa Valley take samples of Chardonnay being aged on the yeast cell residues that develop during barrel fermentation, a process known as "sur lie" *(above)*. The contact with yeast sediment creates a distinctive flavor.

The best French oak barrels are made with wood that has been aged outdoors for several years and then hand split *(left)*. This wood comes from a relatively new forest resource in the Vosges region of northeast France. Wine aged in American oak barrels have a different taste, many experts say, because the wood is usually kiln dried and machine split. With hand-split staves, only about 20 percent of the log will actually be made into a wine barrel. In order to bend moistened oak staves into the form of a tight-fitting barrel, coopers at François Frères in Burgundy burn oak scrap inside the barrel-to-be *(above)*. Later, another fire will "toast" the inside surfaces with enough char to impart a distinctive flavor to the Chardonnay that ages in these barrels.

A portable work lamp illuminates the process of racking, or carefully drawing off clear wine in a way that leaves sediments behind, at the Domaine Drouhin winery in Burgundy *(above)*. The aging cellars at Drouhin date back more than two centuries and at one time were the official repository of the wines owned by the French kings *(top right)*. During that time, it was common to refer to the wine lost to evaporation and tasting as "the angels' share." Chardonnay almost quivers as it is poured into a tasting glass *(right)*.

The glow from a burning stick of sulfur reflects on the face of
Hubert Chavy at his winery in Meursault, France *(left)*. The burning
sulfur fills the empty barrel with sulfur dioxide that prevents
formation of harmful molds and bacteria. "Every harvest is important,"
he says, "because I will make wine only thirty times in my life."
Five Chardonnay samples at an Oregon winery lab are checked for
taste and chemical composition *(above)*.

ise   Ginger   Grass   Green Pepper   Apple   Lime   Kiwi   Lemon   Grapefruit   Orange

Before they are blended into a final mixture to become California sparkling wine, Chardonnay and several other
varieties await sampling by experts for flavor, balance and body *(top left)*. The clarity of these Chardonnay samples in New Zealand
illustrate the different stages of barrel aging *(left)*. As the wine finishes the process, it's typical for the yeasts, oak residue,
and other sediments to settle out to the bottom. Once a week, visitors to Robert Mondavi Winery are offered an introductory
class in the techniques of tasting and recognizing the aromas and flavors that can be present in different wines *(above)*.

Should the flavor of Chardonnay come mainly from the grape or from the barrels? The winemakers' classic debate will probably never end. But the wine from this stainless steel tank near the French village of Chardonnay near Mâcon never sees oak, yet still ranks among the best *(left)*. As with most wines, blending day for Chardonnay at a Napa Valley winery occurs only once a year. It's a critical time when all the barrels await sampling and tasting by a panel of experts from the winery *(above)*. Usually, the winemaker makes the final decision.

Bright backlighting on this bottling line in South Africa highlights any cracks or underfilling of the bottles *(above)*.
Almost dressed for the party, these Champagne bottles in Epernay await their labels *(right)*. Although other sparkling wines may
taste the same and be made from chardonnay grapes, only wines produced in this region of France can be called Champagne.
A traditional Chardonnay-style wineglass takes form at the Riedel Glass factory in Austria *(far right)*.

Each bottle in this French Champagne cellar is
twisted a quarter turn on a regular basis to foster fermentation
in a process called "riddling" *(left)*. All this manual
labor is one reason Champagne-style wines are so expensive.
An inspection light reveals yeast cells settling toward the
mouth of a Champagne bottle *(above)*. Later this sediment will
be frozen and extracted, a "dosage" of wine and sugar will be
added, and a reverse-tapered cork will be forced into the opening
and wired. Concentration and attention to detail are
the hallmark of the wines from Jose Challe at the Pol Roger
Champagne House in Epernay, France *(following page)*.

"This elegant Chardonnay, this global grape, holds domain in the world of wine, whether solo or as the backbone for Champagne."

ANTONIA ALLEGRA
AUTHOR, ST. HELENA, CALIFORNIA

chapter four
CHARDONNAY

the
experience

Beringer Vineyards' century-old Rhine House in St. Helena, where Chardonnay is a premium product, is one
of Napa Valley's most popular attractions *(left)*. On a busy summer day, as many as 800 visitors may sample the wines.
Near the town of Chardonnay, France, Philibert Talbert warmly welcomes visitors to his family winery *(above)*.

Signs of soaring popularity: This street near Santa Maria, California, leads directly to a winery *(above)*. Chardonnay is overwhelmingly featured at the wineries listed on the sign tower in Santa Barbara County, California *(right)*. In New Zealand, Chardonnay is one of the four featured varieties on the preferred wine list *(top right)*; Chardonnay is well represented in the cartoon selection list at a Burgundy wine shop *(far right)*.

Foxen Canyon Wine Trail

COTTONWOOD

RANCHO SISQUOC

FOXEN

BEDFORD & THOMPSON

ZACA MESA

ANDREW MURRAY

FESS PARKER

FIRESTONE

WINE BAR

Summer Rosé	2F	4F
Chardonnay	3F	6F
Pinot Noir	3F	6F
Célèbre	3F	6F

Cassis DE Bourgogne 48 Frs

Prix de la Bouteille

* Cuvée de la Maison Rouge		29F
* Bourgogne Passetoutgrain	1993	34F
* Bourgogne Aligoté	1993	39F
* Bourgogne Pinot Noir	1994	39F
* Bourgogne Chardonnay	1993	45F
* Htes Côtes de Beaune	1992	45F
* Htes Côtes de Nuits	1993	48F
* Saint Véran	1993	55F
* Chorey les Beaune	1991	62F
* Savigny les Beaune	1992/93	68F
* Santenay	1993	70F
* Rully (Rouge)	1992	75F
* Beaune	1992	75F
* Chablis	1994	78F
* Chassagne Montrachet	1992	80F

The cumbersome task of gently twisting Champagne bottles to move sediments
into the neck is being replaced in some wineries by mechanical shakers that are claimed
to do the same job more reliably and at a lower cost *(top)*. Mounted emblems
of exquisite experiences, "plaques de muselet" are the embossed metal logo caps that
were attached to the cork stoppers of the world's best Champagnes *(above)*.
Four miles of Champagne cellars twist under the grounds and mansion of
the Pol Roger Champagne House *(right)*.

Carved casks at the L'Ormarins Estate in South Africa are directly descended from the Huguenot settlers who brought winemaking to the region in 1694 *(above)*. Like most excellent chardonnay-growing regions, these vineyards in the Franschhoek area of South Africa are cooled and moderated by the ocean just a few mountain ridges away *(top right)*. When a hundred-year-old winery in the Stellenbosch region of South Africa was remodeled recently, special attention was given to details including the authentic door handles at the main entrance *(right)*.

Three hands can hardly pour fast enough to satisfy eager participants in a Chardonnay tasting and identification competition in Burgundy *(left)*. An array of professionals in the French wine industry blind-taste various wines at a government research lab in Beaune *(above)*. Don't look for these jobs in the want ads; turnover is low. Symbolizing the dizzying number of styles for making excellent Chardonnay and the more than 3,000 wineries that produce the highly popular wine, this photograph depicts a representative sample of the best Chardonnays available today *(preceding pages)*.

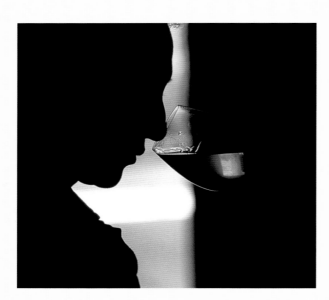

Winemaker Elias Fernandez sniffs and tastes
a wine just before it goes to the bottling line to confirm that
the process of making Shafer Winery's Chardonnay has
achieved his goals *(above)*. A contestant at a wine tasting event
for regional wineries near Château de Meursault in France
swirls a glass of Chardonnay to enhance its aroma *(right)*.
From the tower of the church in the French village of
Fuissé, every field that can be seen is devoted to growing
chardonnay grapes *(following pages)*.

The world's largest charity wine auction, which features some of France's
best Chardonnays, takes place every year in the tiny village of Beaune *(left)*. Don't bid
at the Hospice de Beaune auction if you just want a case of wine. The minimum
quantity is a barrel . . . equivalent to about two dozen cases *(top)*. As soon as bidding begins
on an allotment of wine, a short candle is lit to show the time remaining for
a higher bid to be accepted *(above)*. When a higher bid is received, a second candle is lit,
and the process of lighting candles continues until the wine is auctioned off.

A classic French celebration and spectacle in the village of Chablis is the procession of confreries, ancient organizations of wine lovers. Each year, confreries around the world award friends, new members, and one another with honors that are greatly prized in the winemaking brotherhood *(above)*. The silver cup hanging proudly around this confrere's neck is for tasting. Chardonnay and other wines will pour freely on this one day in the year that the region's best wines and winemakers are honored by their peers *(right)*.

Samples right out of the barrel are served to guests at an
annual tasting in California's Sonoma Valley *(above)*. At Clos du Bois
winery in Sonoma Valley, a 90-foot table will welcome
guests at a dinner that honors those who contributed to the winery's
success *(right)*. With a brash aggressiveness that reflects the way
Chardonnay has seized a commanding share of the world's white wine
market, this retail display of California wines offers brands
that encompass the entire range of winemaking styles practiced
with Chardonnay *(following pages)*.

"Chardonnay is the superstar of this century. Grounded by California, the "new" Americans as an attractive and its success has been